All Kinds of
Animals

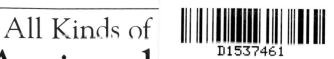

Megan K. Wasp

ABRAMS & COMPANY Publishers, Inc.
Waterbury, CT

Contents

Humans share the Earth with more than a million other animals. Some are as huge as whales. Others are so tiny that we can't see them.

To keep track of all these creatures, scientists put them into groups of animals that are alike.

Humans belong to a group of animals called _mammals_. Mammals have hair or fur on their bodies.

Mammals care for their young. Mothers feed their babies milk and protect them.

Mammals are *warm-blooded.* Their bodies work to stay the same temperature, no matter how hot or cold it is around them.

Giraffes and foxes are mammals. What are some other mammals?

Birds are covered with feathers. Like mammals, they are warm-blooded.

Birds lay eggs. They have two legs and two wings. They also have beaks.

Ostriches and penguins are birds, even though they can't fly. What are some other birds?

Most _fish_ are covered with scales.
They have fins for swimming. They
have gills for breathing underwater.

Like birds, fish lay eggs. But unlike birds, fish are *cold-blooded*. Their body temperature changes with the temperature around them.

Sharks are fish. What are some other fish?

Reptiles also lay eggs and are cold-blooded. But reptiles breathe through lungs.

Reptiles have dry skin covered with scales. Some reptiles even have shells.

Lizards and snakes are reptiles. What are some other reptiles?

Amphibians have smooth, moist skin. Many amphibians live part of their lives in water and part of their lives on land. They are cold-blooded and lay their eggs in water.

Amphibian babies do not look like their parents. They have gills for breathing underwater. Later on, they develop lungs for breathing on land.

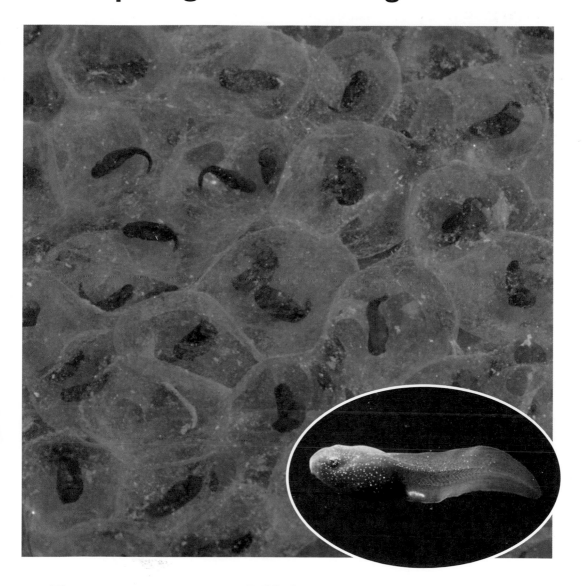

Frogs are amphibians. What are some other amphibians?

Insects have a hard covering on the outside. They have two antennae. Most of them also have wings.

All insects have six legs. They also have three body parts.

Wasps and grasshoppers are insects. What are some other insects?

Be a scientist! Look at each of these animals. To which group does it belong? How can you tell?